YO-BBD-195

Time Out with Jesus

52

Devotions for Christian Teachers

Jacqueline L. Loontjer

CONCORDIA

PUBLISHING HOUSE

Scripture taken from the HOLY BIBLE, NEW INTERNATIONAL VERSION®. Copyright © 1973, 1978, 1984 by International Bible Society. Used by permission of Zondervan Publishing House. All Rights Reserved.

The "NIV" and "New International Version" trademarks are registered in the United States Patent and Trademark Office by International Bible Society. Use of either trademark requires the permission of International Bible Society.

Copyright © 1993 Concordia Publishing House
3558 S. Jefferson Avenue, St. Louis, MO 63118-3968
Manufactured in the United States of America

All rights reserved. No part of this publication may be reproduced, stored in a retrieval system, or transmitted, in any form or by any means, electronic, mechanical, photocopying, recording, or otherwise, without the prior written permission of Concordia Publishing House.

Library of Congress Cataloging-in-Publication Data

Loontjer, Jacqueline L., 1947–
    Time out with Jesus : 52 devotions for the Christian teacher / Jacqueline L. Loontjer.
            p.   cm.
    ISBN 0-570-04611-4
    1. Teachers—Prayer-books and devotions—English. 2. Sunday school teachers—Prayer-books and devotions—English. 3. Devotional calendars. I. Title.
BV4596.T43L66   1993
242'.69—dc20
                                                                          93-2986

---

1 2 3 4 5 6 7 8 9 10 VP 02 01 00 99 98 97 96 95 94 93

For my best friend
and most trusted colleague, Wayne,
who has gone home.

Contents

Tangent Teaching

Reading: Ephesians 2:8–9

By grace you have been saved, through faith—and this not from yourselves, it is the gift of God—not by works, so that no one can boast.

"What is an acrostic, Mrs. Loontjer?" Tom ventured.

We were discussing God's astonishing grace for His people. On the chalkboard, I had written:

God's
Riches
At
Christ's
Expense

I called it an acrostic—and it launched an unplanned, but great, learning experience.

After I answered Tom's question, we created some more acrostics. They became concise, complete statements of faith, like this one from Erica:

Jehovah
Eternally
Saves
Us
Sinners

Or consider the one from David:

Such
Awesome
Victor
Is
Our
Redeemer

Tom's turned out to be:

Love
Our
Redeemer
Daily

Only children who know and love the risen Lord could write such trusting truths. What an edifying event, worked by the Holy Spirit.

"Keep this faith, kids," I whispered.

Prayer:

God, I never cease to marvel at how You work in Your people. You wait for me to be still, and You teach me through my students. Please don't let me lose the capacity to go off on a tangent so my class and I can discover further wonders of Your love. You and I know I learn more with each class. Thanks—I need to be reminded. In Jesus' beautiful name. Amen.

Homework:

Write your own acrostic of faith based on a name for Jesus.

People Prisms

Reading: Matthew 5:16

Let your light shine before men, that they may see your good deeds and praise your Father in heaven.

Prisms fascinate me. When a beam of light shines through these pyramid-shaped pieces of glass, an ordinary room is decorated with the glories of the spectrum.

Teachers can be prisms too. We walk around performing our daily tasks in a rather ordinary fashion. Then, without warning, God's light shines through us and our students are covered with rainbows of God's love.

Some teachers seem to be walking rainbows. They smile; they encourage; they reprove gently; they love, as Christ loves them. Their students flourish in their care because they are growing in Son-light. The children glow with Christ's marvelous light as it splits in the spectrum of their teacher's service.

Mark may need the blue of a peaceful calm as his parents struggle to save their marriage. Cindy looks for the yellow Son-shine of a smile and a hug after a frantic morning at home. José wants the red of a gentle prod about his behavior. Abby hides in the corner until orange warmth draws her into the group. The Son-light is shining on them and they, in turn, become smaller prisms, refracting Christ's light among their friends and at home.

Unfortunately, teachers can also block Christ's illumination, like clouds that only let harmful ultraviolet rays through. Sarcasm and avoidance cast a gray gloom over everyone, and children take that color home also.

Let the Son shine! He will decorate your classroom with caring prisms who split His light rays and shine back on you.

Prayer:

Eternal Light, You only are the source of my brilliance. Shine into my darkened heart and illumine each corner. Shine through my actions so that my students can feel the warmth of Your gentle love. Continue to make us rainbows, adorning each other with Your glow, so others, too, will be "called out of the darkness into the marvelous light." In Your glorious name. Amen.

Homework:
Break up a beam of light with a prism, and reflect on how God's light shines through your teaching.

Jesus, My Mentor

Reading: Luke 6:49

But the one who hears My words and does not put them into practice is like a man who built a house on the ground without a foundation. The moment the torrent struck that house, it collapsed and its destruction was complete.

In the ancient Greek epic *The Odyssey,* Odysseus asked his elderly friend and adviser, Mentor, to serve as guardian of his son, Telemachus. Later, Mentor guided the son as he searched the ancient world for his father.

Today, the word *mentor* is defined as a wise and trusted teacher, guide, and friend. A mentor can be a faithful counselor, calling on years of experience to assist another.

In education circles, the concept of *mentor teachers* is widespread. These experienced, qualified teachers take newer teachers under their wing and help them gain confidence. The mentors guide them as they prepare and execute their lessons. They help them analyze what works and what doesn't. The mentors listen and suggest, but they don't lead by the nose.

We all know teachers whom we admire or pattern ourselves after. We trust their judgment and experience. Furthermore, we respect them as they calmly go about their business of teaching children. Consciously or unconsciously, we model our teaching after theirs.

Jesus is the perfect mentor for Christian teachers. We know Him to be our best friend, one who's always there to listen to our joys and sorrows, our successes and failures. He acts as our guide and guard. We can trust His counseling. He suffered the same temptations and trials we experience, and overcame them for us.

Jesus is the Master Teacher. His parables are unparalleled as teaching tools. His loyalty to His friends went even beyond death. His lessons on the treatment of children are forthright and full of love. Jesus' wisdom fills the universe and surpasses all our problems. And His lessons on forgiveness convey the heart of the Christian faith.

We trust Jesus to lead us as we teach His children. As with all good mentors, He's right there, through the power of God's Word, to assist, recommend, and advise.

Prayer:
Master Teacher, advise me as I prepare to teach. Guide my words and actions in, and out of, the classroom. You taught volumes with Your loving living. Continue to be my wise counselor and friend. Amen.

Homework:
Who is your most trusted mentor? Give that person a call and say thanks.

From Everlasting to Everlasting

Reading: Psalm 118:24–29

This is the day the Lord has made; let us rejoice and be glad in it. O Lord, save us; O Lord, grant us success. Blessed is he who comes in the name of the Lord. From the house of the Lord we bless you. The Lord is God, and He has made His light shine upon us. With boughs in hand, join in the festal procession up to the horns of the altar. You are my God, and I will give You thanks; You are my God, and I will exalt You. Give thanks to the Lord, for He is good; His love endures forever.

Teacher's Agenda
Help from on high
All the preparations and planning
Never alone in the classroom
Kids, over twenty of them
Sing praises and tell sorrows
Give them love and forgiveness
Innocence ruined
Victorious Savior and Friend
Innocence restored
New life through God's grace
Getting love and forgiveness

Invigorating daily challenges
Students' charitable sharing

Eyes, ears, almost always tuned in to you
Verses to memorize and internalize
Endless life of praying
Righteousness of Jesus over us
Little ones, middle ones, bigger ones
After all is said and done—God's peace
Spirit-filled living and loving
The focus: the cross
Illustrations, parables, examples
Never giving up on a student
God never gives up on me, or forsakes me.

Prayer:

You alone, God, deserve thanks and praise, for You alone lavish mercy on me. May my whole life be a gift of thankful service to You. In Your Son's name. Amen.

Homework:

Read Psalm 100 aloud. Choose a verse you find particularly uplifting and memorize it.

Memo to Teachers from Students

Reading: 1 Timothy 4:11–12

Command and teach these things. Don't let anyone look down on you because you are young, but set an example for the believers in speech, in life, in love, in faith and in purity.

You've given the class an assignment that you hope will get them to think. They are to pretend they're getting a new teacher and write some guidelines for that person's teaching. First, they should work in groups to do some brainstorming, and then go to their own desks to start writing.

As you observe them, Tony snickers. You know his paper will say something about all-day recesses and candy and pop for nutrition break. That's his level of development.

Krista chews on her pencil and painfully concentrates. In a minute she'll be at your elbow saying, "I can't think of anything to write." With a few questions, you gently lead her around to some ideas. She brightens up and scurries off to write them down. She'll be back. That's her level of development.

The rest work more or less diligently as you walk around, helping to spell words here and there. You pass Rod's and Cara's desks and see they are carefully considering their words. That's their level of development.

Later, you read the kids' papers and your heart opens. As you read between the lines, you hear some heartfelt cries.

1. Don't correct me in front of people if you can help it. Private talks are better.

2. I won't always give the right answer because I can't express myself very well. Help me.

3. Don't ignore me when I ask questions. I might try to find out from someone else.

4. Don't confuse me by being inconsistent. Say what you mean and then do it.

5. If you make a mistake, it's okay to apologize to me.

6. Don't forget that I need lots of love.

7. Please show me the wonderful love of God in Jesus that brings me forgiveness.

8. Don't do anything that would lead me away from Jesus and His love.

9. Please help me learn to live the Christian way.

I have to ask myself: Am I ready for this level of development?

Prayer:

Dear Father, let me see my teaching from my students' viewpoints. Help me stay true to them as I stay true to You. Don't let me be afraid of changing if it will help my students' learning. In Your Son's name. Amen.

Homework:

Ask your students to write out what they think your objectives for a class were. Did they grasp the objectives you planned?

3 R's

Reading: 1 Peter 3:15

But in your hearts set apart Christ as Lord. Always be prepared to give an answer to everyone who asks you to give the reason for the hope that you have. But do this with gentleness and respect.

My educational clock starts winding on August 1. That clock says, "Only a few more weeks . . . " Or it may say frantically, "Only a few more days!" Whether you teach in a parochial school, public school, or Sunday school, your fall schedule is about to return.

The clock's voice may sound plaintively as you think back to the weeks just past and you or your family's time for rest and rejuvenation. Summers are true blessings.

What did you do with your blessing? Some people take classes; some take extended trips; some paint their houses; some write books or articles; some teach their own children how to cook; some renew old friendships and make new ones. God energizes us with a change of routine.

But it's August and the frantic voice intrudes now and then. What can you do with the last days of summer? Your clock is telling you to gear up for the months to come.

For Christian teachers the summer months have a two-fold purpose. Yes, we rest and rejuvenate. That's a given. But we also have time for reflection on our service to the Lord. We think back to former classes and pray that their knowledge may be strong enough to carry them forward. More than that, we pray for the Holy Spirit to keep their faith strong enough to see them through any temptations.

We also think ahead to the coming class, and pray for them. We pray for the Spirit's guidance in our preparations. We ask for an extra measure of patience for whatever teacher-testing times will come. We request inquisitive, eager students to challenge us. But mostly, we beseech God in Jesus' name to forgive our past failures and continue to use us as leaders in His kingdom.

Rest—rejuvenation—reflection. How are your 3 R's? Your educational and eternal clocks are ticking.

Prayer:

Lord Jesus Christ, during Your earthly life You too labored within the limitations of hours, days, and seasons. Help me use the precious commodity of time to work in Your kingdom. Give me adequate periods of rest for body and soul, so my teaching won't suffer. In Your name. Amen.

Homework:

As you prepare for your busy times, be sure to schedule time for God. Use that time for prayer and meditation on His Word.

By Faith

Reading: Hebrews 11:13–16

All these people were still living by faith when they died. They did not receive the things promised; they only saw them and welcomed them from a distance. And they admitted that they were aliens and strangers on earth. People who say such things show that they are looking for a country of their own. If they had been thinking of the country they had left, they would have had opportunity to return. Instead, they were longing for a better country—a heavenly one. Therefore God is not ashamed to be called their God, for He has prepared a city for them.

God's servants—we all wear that name. To do so puts us in awesome company. As we quickly skim the eleventh chapter of Hebrews, we see example after example of people whose faith remained steadfast as God guided them through unbelievable testings.

Noah, Abraham, and the rest were all God's servants and He asked them to do difficult things. It's not easy to continue working on a huge boat for years—in a desert, no less—when the neighbors are jeering. It's not easy to raise the knife and prepare to sacrifice your son and heir. It's not easy to give up a life of ease and luxury in an Egyptian palace and live as a Hebrew slave.

But each of the people mentioned in Hebrews 11 walked the path God chose for them, praying to avoid sin's potholes along the way. They trusted God's loving providence. They knew God was leading them.

Now, thousands of years later, we are God's chosen servants. God doesn't give us a set of blueprints to follow, as He did for Noah. We don't have face-to-face talks with God, as did Abraham. And we don't follow a pillar of fire or cloud, like Moses. But in Christ, God is present with us and is involved with us in an even more personal way.

God strengthens our faith. He knows it isn't easy to remain patient when the same student keeps disrupting the class. He knows the hours we put into preparation and follow-up could be used in other ways. He knows it's easy to carry our burdens on our sleeves.

So God sticks with us in all situations and gives us encouragement through the people He has placed around us. More importantly, He speaks to us in His Word and Sacraments, and— yes—He does answer prayers.

Why do we continue teaching, even though the hours are long and the rewards not always apparent? Go back to Hebrews 11:16. "Instead, they were longing for a better country—a heavenly one. Therefore God is not ashamed to be called their God, for He has prepared a city for them."

What other reason do we need?

Prayer:

Eternal, immovable God, keep me close to You through whatever testings come my way. When You speak to me in Word and Sacrament, enable me to hear Your will for me. Let no obstacle prevent me from following You. Through Jesus' name. Amen.

Homework:

Choose your favorite Old Testament character mentioned in Hebrews 11 and re-read his or her story. Concentrate on all the instances of faith-challenging tests. Pray for such a faith.

Junk Drawers

Reading: Hebrews 10:21–24

And since we have a great priest over the house of God, let us draw near to God with a sincere heart in full assurance of faith, having our hearts sprinkled to cleanse us from a guilty conscience and having our bodies washed with pure water. Let us hold unswervingly to the hope we profess, for He who promised is faithful. And let us consider how we may spur one another on toward love and good deeds.

God doesn't make junk! We often see this saying proclaimed on T-shirts and posters.

I thought of those words as I started cleaning my junk drawer. You know the kind of drawer I mean. It has a multitude of objects "that I might need someday." Only when that day comes, they can't be found amid the other junk.

I sorted through paper clips and rubber bands, out-of-date coupons and toys from fast-food restaurants. I found a long-lost gas bill receipt. My mother's recipe for potato salad turned up. A dozen dry pens got thrown away, but two dozen were kept! Twelve of my daughter's barrettes were there, as well as the tie my son "lost." "God may not make junk, but people can sure collect an assortment of man-made stuff," I muttered. "I also know now why adults don't buy those T-shirts. They don't have room to keep them!"

We may be tempted to keep a mental junk drawer with our students. I mean mentally filing away incidents with a certain student that get dredged up weeks later to support the "you-always-do-this" claim. We teach our students that God forgives their sin and does not hold it against them, but, like an elephant, some teachers never forget.

Yes, it is helpful to keep anecdotal records on our students, but we need to be fair. We can use them to discuss improvement or areas that need extra help, but we should not throw them in the student's face at times when we lose patience. Instead, as in Hebrews 10:24, "Let us consider how we may spur one another on toward love and good deeds."

Thanks be to God that He doesn't bring out our past records every time we pray. If He did, asking for forgiveness would be an exercise in futility. No, He cleans our slates and because of Jesus He does not hold our sins against us. He doesn't file a 3 × 5 card for each sin. Heaven couldn't hold them all!

God hates sin, yes, but in Christ He loves us sinners. Can we do less? Don't fill your mental file drawers with past offenses. Let your students feel God's love for them as you forgive completely.

God made you and each of your students, and He does not make junk!

Prayer:
Forgiving God, forgive me when I act unforgivingly toward my students. Don't let me block Your forgiveness to them. Help me live as a forgiven sinner, a saint who loves the Lord and His charges. Through Jesus. Amen.

Homework:
Look at your student list or anecdotal records. Write something positive about each student.

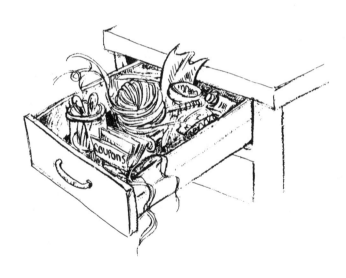

Teacher's Guide

Reading: James 1:22

Do not merely listen to the word, and so deceive yourselves.
Do what it says.

"Where is the teacher's guide?" It was just about time for Sunday school to begin, and I couldn't find the teacher's manual.

Substitute teaching is tough enough when there are clear instructions left by a teacher who knows he or she will be gone. But I had been called to substitute for a teacher who became ill. So here I was, trying to follow someone else's routine and plans. And the teacher's manual was missing!

The secret of subbing is to pretend you're in control, no matter what happens. If the students sense that you're wavering, they'll take advantage of you in a big way! I could feel the vibrations build as the kids watched me. I probably could get by without the manual, but how?

"Oh, please, God, help me," I whispered as I put on my best calm, professional smile.

He did, of course. He directed my thoughts to the best teacher's guide, the Bible. The sixth- graders were a bit intrigued when I told them to put away their lesson books. We were only going to use their Bibles. They figured my plans would crack.

I started the impromptu lesson with Psalm 119:105 and we discussed how God's Word lights our path, leading us through the world's darkness. Isn't that the function of light?

Then we moved on to John 8:12, where Jesus calls Himself the "light of the world," the one necessary for our eternal survival. He came to die, rise, and light our way to heaven's radiance. Donna spoke up and reminded us of Jesus' transfiguration, when "His appearance was like lightning," and the students agreed that lightning makes the worst storm as bright as day.

Finally, we read Matthew 5:14 and Ephesians 5:8, where God tells us that we ourselves are lights. We discussed Jesus' example of not being able to hide a city's lights. We finished with how we modern Christians, "walk as children of light." The kids reported having to make tough decisions as Christian children in a Satan-saturated world. But they knew the light of Jesus shines through them.

I said a silent thanks to God for a Bible with a concordance. The allotted time wasn't up, but, hey, who says Sunday school kids can't have a recess? After all, the Son was shining.

Prayer:
Dear Heavenly Light, illumine my soul. Burst into my entire being with Your brilliance so that I shine forth to my students. Let them also reflect Your lightning love. When sin dims our Gospel light, bring us to repentance. Rekindle our flickerings to be a steady glow. Through Your radiant, redemptive name. Amen.

Homework:
Try to go through a day with only natural lighting. Then think how difficult living without God's light would be.

A Dose a Day

Reading: Galatians 5:13–14

You, my brothers, were called to be free. But do not use your freedom to indulge the sinful nature; rather, serve one another in love. The entire law is summed up in a single command: "Love your neighbor as yourself."

A, B_1, B_2, B_6, B_{12}, C, D, . . . We recognize these letters as vitamins that our bodies need to stay healthy. We make sure our children get them from infancy on, and we know we have more vitality when we take them. Some of us even overdo it in efforts to avoid certain maladies. For instance, vitamin C sales go way up in the fall and winter as people try to ward off colds.

Christian teachers also have a batch of specialized vitamins to tap into each day. The designations are T, I_1, R, I_2, P, and S. They come directly from our God. We just open His container, the Bible, and receive the dosage we need.

The T stands for Truth. We know the truth of salvation and share the prescription with others. I_1 is for Inspiration. We look to God's inspired Word to inspire us in our teaching. R is the vitamin of renewal. Our lives are renewed in Christ daily as we remember our Baptism and receive God's forgiveness. I_2 brings us innovation. God helps us to be innovative as we present our lessons, so that our students become excited about what God has done for them. P is our source of power. Christian teaching can be draining as we give of ourselves to many people. But God provides us with vitamin P through Bible study, His Sacraments, and prayer. The last letter, S, is for set apart. We, as teachers, have been set apart to do a special job for God. We use all the other vitamins to fulfill our calling in His service.

Now, if we reverse these letters, we find the true source of our vitality—the Spirit. God's Holy Spirit keeps us healthy in our faith. Each day He diagnoses our ailments and gives us an abundance of spiritual nutrients to see us through our challenges.

So open up your container. There's no childproof packaging to get in the way. Let the Spirit lead you into God's Word and prayer as you celebrate your God-given vitality.

Prayer:

Dear Holy Spirit, come into my heart and fill my soul with the strength I need to do what You have set before me. Only You can restore my faith and lead me through the many challenges of my day. Fill me with Your love so that it spills over onto my students. In Jesus' name. Amen.

Homework:

Draw a picture of a large bottle of pills. On each pill write the name of a "vitamin" you need in your teaching.

Compassion

Bible Reading: Colossians 3:12–14

Therefore, as God's chosen people, holy and dearly loved, clothe yourselves with compassion, kindness, humility, gentleness and patience. Bear with each other and forgive whatever grievances you may have against one another. Forgive as the Lord forgave you. And over all these virtues put on love, which binds them all together in perfect unity.

Oh, what I learn from my students!

I wanted the junior high Bible study to help the kids care more about other people's problems than about their own—a difficult task for many their age. Young people can get so wrapped up in their cocoons of fear and guilt that it's difficult to break free.

We were studying Colossians 3:12–14, where Paul tells us how "God's chosen people" are to act. The students understood kindness and gentleness, but they wanted to reserve patience for parent and teacher use. They had a hard time with humility; after all, our society does not teach us to be humble. Love and forgiveness were seen as "what God does for us," but forgiving one another was an uncomfortable idea. Then we came to compassion.

Compassion is hard for adults to comprehend since it involves a mixture of love, pity, kindness, and wanting to help someone else. As the class floundered with this concept, my mind raced to find something they could latch onto. Then I remembered the old Native American proverb: Before you judge someone, walk a mile in his moccasins. Maybe a role-playing session would help.

I explained the proverb and told the students I wanted them to switch shoes with someone for 10 minutes. They were to become that person and feel or react to things as that individual would. They looked at me as only junior highers can when they think an adult has completely gone over the edge. They reluctantly agreed—because I was the teacher.

Ten minutes later, a thoughtful group reclaimed their shoes and, once again, tried to define compassion. Their eyes had been opened to their treatment of others.

Eric said, "Compassion means to go past what you see on the person's exterior and find the real interior person who needs your caring and understanding. Then you can truly see what will help that person."

These junior high kids challenged each other to find an individual that week "to change shoes with." Even their parents and siblings were eligible! The best part was that they planned to do it as anonymously as possible. We prayed, and we all went out to practice compassion.

Prayer:

Dear Lord, You have had compassion for me from the beginning of time. You became a man and walked in my sandals, so that I can be forgiven. Help my students and me to walk in Your sandals, showing Your love to whomever we meet. In Your name. Amen.

Homework:

Identify a hurting student, parent, or colleague. Anonymously, do something that will ease that person's pain.

A Christian Teacher's Calendar

Reading: Psalm 31:14–16

But I trust in You, O Lord; I say, "You are my God." My times are in Your hands; deliver me from my enemies and from those who pursue me. Let Your face shine on Your servant; save me in Your unfailing love.

A teacher's calendar is not like other folks'. In December when other people are doing their end-of-the-year inventories and accountings, we are smack in the middle of our responsibilities. In June, when we're doing our wrap-up, other workers are right in the center of their production year.

A further look at a Christian teacher's calendar shows:

• August: We pray for God's guidance as we prepare for a new class, and we get more and more eager to meet them and get started.

- September: Now we can get into it. The students learn what we expect, and we learn what to expect from each of them. God, help those two things to coincide.

- October: This month brings spectacular color changes in nature and days of Indian summer. We're getting to know our children and their families, and their special needs. Help us all, God.

- November: As cold weather closes in, we think of people in need. We teach Christian love and responsibility as we help our class sponsor food and clothing drives. Thank You, God, for all our blessings.

- December: In this month when we celebrate the birth of our Prince of Peace, things seem far from peaceful! Decorations, making gifts, practicing songs and recitations . . . Happy birthday, Jesus, and help us keep our activities in proper focus.

- January: A new calendar year begins. We make and then break resolutions. We think about new beginnings. Help me use my time wisely, Lord.

- February: Valentines fill the children with excitement. Jesus, fill our hearts with Your love.

- March: Spring signs begin to appear. It's Lent and we repent of our sins which sent God's Son to Calvary.

- April: Nature gives us a never-ending show as rainstorms and sunshine trade off, and flowers sprout to life again. They're a reflection of Your Easter glory, Christ.

- May: We can feel the school year winding down and there's a sad anticipation—not in the students, of course! Keep them in Your care, Lord.

- June: Have a great summer, teacher. Another year is finished. Thank You for helping me, God.

- July: Ah, yes, rest. Revive me for more service to You, God.

Prayer:

My times are in Your hands. Focus my attention on the way You want my time spent, Lord. Help me schedule my time so that I always serve You most effectively. Amen.

Homework:

Look back through your appointment book or calendar and reflect on the past year. What do you think God wants you to add or subtract from your schedule?

R and R

Reading: Psalm 62:5–8

Find rest, O my soul, in God alone; my hope comes from Him. He alone is my rock and my salvation; He is my fortress, I will not be shaken. My salvation and my honor depend on God; He is my mighty rock, my refuge. Trust in Him at all times, O people; pour out your hearts to Him, for God is our refuge.

Fantastic! Gorgeous! Breathtaking! My senses revelled in the sights. I was standing on the balcony of the condominium where my husband and I were vacationing. The view was wonderful, and I couldn't get enough of it. The lake reflected the azure color of the sky. The feathery clouds above seemed to be repeated in the wildflowers peeking out from under the winter's brown.

Ah, R and R! Isn't it great? We needed it! It had been a long winter trying to keep up with our schedules and our two children's. So we arranged a week-end of rest and recreation—thanks to some terrific grandparents.

Sleeping late . . . walks by the lake . . . leisurely shopping . . . no phone calls . . . no cooking, and even better, no dishes to do . . . Just letting the relaxation seep through our muscles and into our bones. No hassles . . . no headaches . . . no heading opposite directions.

Thank You, God, for times like this, I breathed.

As I stood there, R and R took on a new meaning for me. Reflection and renewal seemed more fitting than rest and relaxation. I reflected on God's marvelous creation and His preservation of the whole world. This all-powerful Being loves me, of all things, and He chose me to spread His message of love to children. He also cares that I get tired, and He leads me to periods of renewal.

My thoughts turned to my students. They need to revel in God's love also, come to Him in repentance, and feel the joy of His forgiveness. God is using ME to lead them to Him.

Now I understood. God gave me this weekend for recommitment and recommissioning.

Returning home, I smiled at a gray squirrel scurrying from branch to branch. My hurry was the same. But now, thanks to my Righteous Redeemer, I was ready and raring to go!

Prayer:

Dear Creator, Redeemer, and Sanctifier, I can't praise You enough for all You've done for me. Keep Your goodness before me as a guide, Your support beneath me as a safety net, and Your command to "feed My lambs" my primary purpose for teaching. To You alone belongs the glory! Amen.

Homework:

Besides teaching, what do you enjoy doing the best? So, go do it!

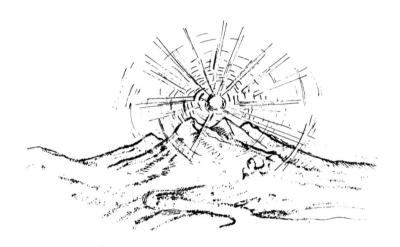

Serving Together

Reading: Colossians 3:23–24

Whatever you do, work at it with all your heart, as working for the Lord, not for men, since you know that you will receive an inheritance from the Lord as a reward. It is the Lord Christ you are serving.

Classifying people has reached an impersonal and disturbing level in our age of polls and computer categorizing. If an organization wants to discover the feelings of a specific group, they punch in a certain set of codes and the microchips print out an appropriate list. Names can be categorized by age, gender, race, address, or any combination of things.

We have classifications in church work also. An obvious one is that of educational degrees. But not everyone laboring in the church has letters behind his or her name. The categories can be subtle.

Let's start with the neutral category of coworkers. This category covers everyone from pastor to janitor. It implies a parallel effort, but can describe people who do different tasks. In other words, one may preach the sermon, while someone else types the newsletter. Or one may teach Sunday school, but someone else may clean the floors. This term implies unity in working for the Lord, but allows for a diversity of jobs.

Next, we have the level of colleagues. These people work at the same tasks—they might teach Sunday school or staff the day care center. They may have unity among themselves, but their group usually doesn't include church workers who perform different tasks. And even these people may not be unified in their way of thinking about God's work.

I like the term *comrade.* The dictionary defines a comrade as a friend or close companion. When a church's members truly "work at it with all [their] heart, as working for the Lord" (Colossians 3:23), it is less likely that divisions, subtle or stated, will occur. Volunteers will feel appreciated, as will paid workers. Custodians will clean to the best of their ability. Secretaries will answer the phone with joy. Teachers carry out their share of God's tasks willingly.

How do we move from coworkers to comrades? We ask the Holy Spirit to help us keep our eyes on our leader: our Lord Jesus. He leads us all in one direction—to heaven—and He also aligns us in the same direction along the way.

With Jesus' example as our unifier, we are comrades in Christ's company.

Prayer:

Father God, You never desired division in Your world. Your creation was perfectly harmonious, but sin destroyed it. You want Your one holy, Christian church to be united in truth. Help me promote unity in many small ways. Let me work in peace with my Christian comrades. On Christ's perfection I depend. Amen.

Homework:

Read Galatians 3:26–29. In your teaching, how can you heal divisiveness? Start on it today, with God's help.

Daffodils, Daisies, and Dandelions

Reading: Psalm 8:1

O Lord, our Lord, how majestic is Your name in all the earth! You have set Your glory above the heavens.

"God's country." People sometimes refer to mountainous regions when they use these words. Those scenes are majestic and awe-inspiring, but I think God's favorite places might be flower gardens. Why else did He take such exquisite care when He created the amazing variety of blossoms?

From the blazing oranges of tiger lilies to the pale pinks of baby roses, from the deep purples of iris to the pale lavenders of alyssum, from the sunny daffodils to the profusion of peonies, you know flowers teach us something about God's glory. He gave us the shy moss roses and pansies, the delicacy of orchids, and the hardiness of sunflowers. Even if people never planted cultured flowers, He has painted the world with wildflowers.

God loves children in the same way. The proliferation of flowers is minor compared to individual children. Each child is unique—and, oh, so beautiful.

In any class you may have tulips, the early bloomers who come in ready to go. You may find the happy daisy faces of eagerness. There may be the shy violets who need your warmth to bloom. You will find the tough geraniums who just keep blooming and growing. Of course, you will have some thorny roses, beautiful but difficult to handle. None of your students are dandelions that need to be weeded out.

God loves His children, young and old. He created us, and, more importantly, He redeemed us in Jesus Christ. Sin separates us from Him, but He leads us to repentance and forgives us totally. As any gardener knows, though, weeds keep coming up. Sin is the same way, and God removes our sins each time we ask.

"O Lord, our Lord, how majestic is Your name in all the earth!" (Psalm 8:1). Christian teachers are caretakers of God's precious garden. We look to Him for help in nurturing the tender shoots growing there.

Prayer:
Creator of the vast universe and the tiniest flower, teach this teacher the infinite value of Your growing garden of children. Keep me from treading on them, and guide me as I nurture their growth. Water us, fertilize us, and help us all grow toward the Son. In Jesus' love and grace. Amen.

Homework:
Ask students to name flowers suited to their personalities. Make some paper flowers for a bulletin board and put their pictures in the centers.

The Insect Class

Reading: Proverbs 30:25

Ants are creatures of little strength, yet they store up their food in the summer.

"Jason, you're bugging me!" warns the teacher. Jason has learned that "bugging" someone is not a good thing, so he takes the warning to heart and quits that behavior.

Bugs have a bad image. They are seen by many people as undesirable parts of God's creation. But scientists know they are necessary to the food web God planned.

Students also have a bad image to some people. They may regard students as tax burdens or worse.

I see some parallels between insects and students. First, we have the pest category. Mosquitoes and flies seem to have no worthwhile purpose. They carry diseases and bother us endlessly. Students in this category are constantly irritating someone with little jabs—verbal or otherwise. It's easy to see only the surface behavior and miss the fact that they're practically screaming for someone's attention. They have probably learned at home that negative behavior brings attention of some kind. Pray with and for these children and help them feel Christ's love.

Another class of students resemble grasshoppers and fireflies. They hop from one project to the next, never sticking with one for very long. But they will display wonderful flashes of brilliance at unexpected times. Pray with and for these children—and teach them to be organized.

Ladybugs and bees move busily, doing their God-appointed jobs well. The end products of their work are very satisfying. Students in this category are dependable, learning, and maturing. Pray with and for these children to have continued success.

Last we have the ants. They scurry around, working hard to ward off winter's starvation. Our ants in class are the mature, self-reliant ones who not only do well from day to day, but also plan for the future. School is a time of preparation for following God's plan for their lives. They take advantage of every learning opportunity. Pray with and for these children to keep God in the center of their plans.

Prayer:
Dear God, when young people seem exasperating to me, let me see You in them. Shine through their eyes so that I recognize their vulnerabilities and needs. Keep me focused on bringing them closer to You. In our Savior's name. Amen.

Homework:
Read an article or book on motivating students. Apply useful techniques in the light of your Christian principles.

Unique, but United

Reading: 1 Corinthians 12:12–13

The body is a unit, though it is made up of many parts; and though all its parts are many, they form one body. So it is with Christ. For we were all baptized by one Spirit into one body—whether Jews or Greeks, slave or free—and we were all given the one Spirit to drink.

Jesus loves the little children,
All the children of the world.
Red and yellow, black and white,
They are precious in His sight.
Jesus loves the little children of the world.

And their parents and their siblings and their teachers and . . .

That song lays it all on the line for us as Christian teachers. Jesus loves everyone.

Our schools and Sunday schools are blessed with a diverse group of people: children from black families and white families; children of Hispanic, European, and Asian heritage. Students' parents are pastors, policemen, doctors, assembly-line workers, business people, teachers, and lawyers. The children come from one-parent or two-parent homes, or maybe they're living with their grandparents. We work with athletic, artistic, and dramatic students. Some children are extremely intelligent and use their intelligence wisely. Some are intelligent but don't use their gift. Some are intelligent but need help dealing with learning disabilities. ALL of these children are blessings from God.

How do we, as teachers, bring out the best of each of these individuals—students and their parents—and make them an integral part of the church family?

"We were all baptized by one Spirit into one body" (1 Corinthians 12:13). That's where we start—by recognizing each person as a vital part of the body of Christ. No matter what our function in that body, the whole body suffers if one section is hurt. We talk with our students and their parents and learn their strengths and needs. And God builds the unified body He desires as we—each man, woman, and child—worship at the foot of the same cross and celebrate our unity in Christ despite our differences.

Prayer:

Dear God, You created and love each of us in our own uniqueness. You have brought us to a living faith through Baptism into the same Savior. Unite us in our goals so that all we do builds up our church family, to Your glory and for the children's good. In Christ. Amen.

Homework:

Draw a simple body shape and write the names of fellow staff members on parts of this body. Can you really do without the foot or the fingers?

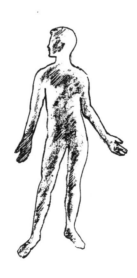

Instant Results

Reading: Psalm 27:14

Wait for the Lord; be strong and take heart and wait for the Lord.

I am not a good wait-er. I never have been. Standing in lines is not my idea of a good time; slow service in a restaurant sets my fingers tapping; and being caught in a parking lot that's supposed to be a freeway makes me very nervous.

To make matters worse, this generation of students is proving to be an instant-gratification lot. Maybe it starts with Sesame Street, and its 15 or 30-second lessons, and continues with television shows that solve everyone's problem in 30 or 60 minutes. Now students expect 60-second service at the hamburger stand. How are they going to sit still for a 45-minute lesson that does not have the pizazz of a television commercial?

It has taken 40-some years, but I can finally see the value of waiting. Maybe the passing years make me want time to go slower, but for whatever reason, I can finally understand Psalm 27:14.

For example, my husband and I wanted to marry after our junior year of college, but God intervened through our parents. He knew it would have been almost impossible to earn living expenses, and our classwork would have suffered. In the first congregation that called us to be day school teachers, we planned to charge in and use our "expertise" to change things. Thank goodness for a patient pastor and principal. We served there for 18 years and saw a lot of changes, but at God's pace.

I was going to teach for two years, then start our family. Instead, I lived through a painful experience because God had other plans. Now we have two wonderful adopted children that couldn't be more ours if they had been born to us naturallly.

When my husband became principal, we figured we'd stay in one place forever. God must have shaken His head at that. Three years later we received a job offer closer to our families, with a new set of challenges. I think you get the picture.

Waiting on God's will is easier now because I know He's there to care for me as I wait. He comforts me and gently leads me as

He reveals His plan for my life. Slowly—ever so slowly—I am learning patience and acceptance.

"Wait for the Lord; be strong and take heart and wait for the Lord" (Psalm 27:14). His timetable is best.

Prayer:

Dear God, a day in our time is merely an instant in Your eternal timeframe. Teach me to wait on Your will. I too often want things to happen in my way and according to my schedule. Remind me that the world works at Your ordinance. In Your Son's name. Amen.

Homework:

Make a list of all the "instants" you enjoy—pudding, rice, fast foods, etc. Ask God to make you a patient waiter in the midst of all this convenience.

Morning Shower

Reading: Romans 6:3–4

Don't you know that all of us who were baptized into Christ Jesus were baptized into His death? We were therefore buried with Him through baptism into death in order that, just as Christ was raised from the dead through the glory of the Father, we too may live a new life.

As I stood there with the warm water pelting me, I slowly came back to life. Getting up early can be a shock to one's system. You collapse wearily the night before and fall into a deep, exhausted sleep. Then before you feel well-rested, the dreaded alarm goes off and you drag yourself out again.

That's why my morning shower is so necessary. It's like push starting an old car—you have to get the sparkplugs sparking so the engine will turn over. The water keeps working on me until my brain and body work in sync, somewhat.

I don't remember exactly when it started, but shower time has become one of my morning prayer times. It may have begun as a groan for help: "Please help me wake up, Lord." But it has slowly evolved into a very private time with God. I lay my sins and daily concerns on Him.

I guess this is my own personal time of being "buried with Him through Baptism" each morning so that I can rise with Him to new life. I am washing away my sins and worries as I pray in Jesus' name, just as I am washing off my daily collection of dry skin and soil.

Christ calls us to think of our Baptism each day, so that we remember all that He has done for us. It is impossible to hide anything from God in the shower. I pray about all my sins—even those pet ones I often rationalize away. I pray for patience and strength with my class. I pray that the Holy Spirit will guide my thoughts, words, and gestures.

Now, on to the next thing I need to do today . . .

Prayer:
Dear Holy Spirit, each morning You bring me to the heavenly throne in repentance. Don't let me be too groggy to pray for complete forgiveness, especially for the sins I commit against my students. In the name of Jesus, whose blood washes away my sins. Amen.

Homework:
Each time you wash today, ask God to remind you that in Baptism, Jesus' blood acts as soul-soap and washes away all your sins.

Sour to Sweet

Reading: Hebrews 11:1

Now faith is being sure of what we hope for and certain of what we do not see.

"Why, Mrs. Loontjer, why?" Latisha demanded. "If God knew His people were going to sin, why did He put that tree in the garden?"

There it was again, a child's preemptory inquisitiveness. This same question comes up each year as we study God's plan of salvation. It joins a host of other questions. How can God not have a beginning or an end? If Jesus is one with the Father and the Spirit, why did only He die? Why doesn't my father believe in God? How can God be everywhere in the world at the same time?

How do I answer my students in terms they can understand? Some of the questions are ones that theologians more learned than I have debated for centuries.

I tell the class, "I have that on my list of questions to ask God when I see Him face-to-face. There are some things we accept only on faith."

But back to our original question about sin. "I was told once that God didn't create robots," I told Latisha. "That's why He gave Adam and Eve free choice in the garden." Latisha smiled, because she could relate to the difference between robots and people. Then we talked about God's love for Adam and Eve, and for us, and His plan for salvation.

When the light dawned on Latisha's face, I knew she had made a personal discovery of faith. "It's like God took the sour fruit of sin and changed it into sweet jelly through Jesus' resurrection," she said. "We are supposed to spread this jelly all over the bread of our lives."

41

Prayer:

Triune God, be with this Christian teacher as I struggle to help children understand You, if only in a minute way. Make my own faith strong and my thoughts humble to recognize Your work in me. In the Son's name. Amen.

Homework:

Sing the words to the children's song "Jesus Loves Me." It says all we need to believe to have eternal life.

Lollipops, Lessons, and Love-Listening

Reading: James 1:19–20

My dear brothers, take note of this: Everyone should be quick to listen, slow to speak and slow to become angry, for man's anger does not bring about the righteous life that God desires.

Tongue twisters are such fun for children.

- *Six slick slimy snakes slid slowly southward.*
- *Peter Piper picked a peck of pickled peppers.*
- *And, of course, there's the famous woodchuck chucking wood . . .*

What's the point? The point is that the tongue twister "lollipops, lessons, and love-listening" can be used to remind us how to relate to our pupils. This short phrase packs a wallop.

Lollipops stand for examples of positive ways we praise children for their efforts. There are so many possible "lollipops" to use: stickers, hugs, candy, pats on the back, public praise, private encouragement, notes home to parents, special privileges. These, and more, tell children we're proud of the progress they're making. Lollipops are well worth the extra time or expense. Just watch your students' faces.

But lollipops are only the dessert! Lessons are the main course. We get ready for a lesson in the way we prepare a special meal for guests. We tease the palate with the introduction. The next serving may be a brief review to tie this lesson to a prior one. Then we get into the meat of it: a substantial concept, something our students' minds can chew on and digest.

Last, our love-listening is like after-dinner coffee. Now our students communicate with us. We listen as Christ listens, with love and acceptance. Our students long for our attention and an appropriate, loving response. An absent-minded "That's nice" doesn't do it. Our love-ears aren't tuned in, and the kids know it.

Go! Use God's gifts to gain guys and gals galore who gladly glorify the gift of God's Son.

Prayer:
Father, You created communication and made it a two-way street. I too often botch it. Tune me in to my students so that I listen lovingly, just as You listen to me. In the name of Jesus. Amen.

Homework:
Think about your own teaching challenges and make up a short tongue twister to help you stay on target.

Changing Seasons

Reading: Ecclesiastes 3:1

There is a time for everything, and a season for every activity under heaven.

How apt, especially in a classroom.

Fall: This time of year brings red apples and orange pumpkins, tart cider and tangy pumpkin pies. Vast amounts of gold and rust-colored leaves become soft hills for jumping onto. The air's temperature changes from warm to crisp to cold. Soccer and football games take the forefront, and classes—preschool to graduate school—get into gear. We greet new students who are timid or questioning or challenging.

Winter: Nature's colors change to whites and blue-grays. The first snowfall inspires children to build snowmen and snowforts, and they try to catch snowflakes on their tongues. People hurry through snow and slush on their various tasks. Christmas brings excitement, busy preparations, and the wonder of celebrating Christ's birth. By now we have developed a sense of real camaraderie with our students.

Spring: Ah, yes! God's encouragement to a static environment comes next. Tiny green sprouts appear all around, promising pinks, yellows, and purples to follow. Our classes anxiously anticipate the sunshine to warm up their world so they can be outside more often. In nature, so many things are beginning, but a teacher's emotions are sadly tinged with the coming separation. In the middle, though, we triumphantly celebrate Easter, when God emphatically said no to sin and yes to forgiven sinners.

Summer: Spring starts a mad downhill rush to the end. Baseball, swimming, and picnics now abound, and the last day of school, or our final meeting with a Sunday school class, arrives. Students and teachers sense freedom and relief, tinged with sadness. One more year is behind them. Just before they rush out into the summer sunshine, some students return for one more hug of reassurance. Then they move on to another year and another teacher, in the cycle of seasons.

Prayer:

Creator, keep me ever mindful of the passing time. Help me never miss an opportunity to present Your love and forgiveness. Bring me and my students to spend eternity with You, where the seasons never change. Through my unchanging Savior. Amen.

Homework:

What season are you experiencing now? List all the blessings that can only be appreciated in this season.

45

ABC's of Christian Teaching

Reading: Ephesians 4:11–13

It was He who gave some to be apostles, some to be prophets, some to be evangelists, and some to be pastors and teachers, to prepare God's people for works of service, so that the body of Christ may be built up until we all reach unity in the faith and in the knowledge of the Son of God and become mature, attaining to the whole measure of the fullness of Christ.

Alphabet, Adam and Eve, apples for the teacher.
Books, boys, the beauty of God's world.
Cleansing, creation, Christ's cross.
Drawing, devotions, daily bread.
Emotions, extra hours, Easter.
Faces, Fig Newtons, forgiveness.
Growing, girls, grace from God.
Happiness, heaven, Holy Spirit.
Ink, inquiry, Immanuel.
Joy, jelly and peanut butter, Jesus' love.
Kids and their King.
Love from the Lord and each other.
Monkeyshines and memory work.
New blue jeans, New Testament, newness of life.
Old Testament prophecies and His open arms.
Preparation and power from God.
Questions, quiet time, quickening of faith.
Rhymes, reading, Redeemer.
Service, singing, Savior.
Time, talents, treasure, truth.
Undeserved love and understanding.
Values and victory over sin.
Whispers, wondering, and the Way.
E**x**pectation and exaltation.
Yellow crayons, yelling youngsters, and yes to prayers.
Zeal and Zion.

Dear Creator of students and teachers, be with me in my teaching and show me Your hand in all I do. Keep me focused on You so my preparation and teaching will share Your love. You alone deserve my eternal praises, for You are my beginning and end, my Alpha and Omega. Amen.

Homework:
Choose one letter of the alphabet and see how many blessings you have been given that start with that letter.

Send, Share, and Sacrifice

Reading: 1 John 4:10

This is love: not that we loved God, but that He loved us and sent His Son as an atoning sacrifice for our sins.

The three R's of education are ever before us: Reading, 'riting, and 'rithmetic. These days we'd probably modify them to R, W, M, and CS: Reading, Writing, Math, and Computer Science. But do you know the three S's? They come directly from our Lord's lesson plans. He teaches us through His hands-on, one-to-one demonstration of *sending, sharing,* and *sacrificing.*

God created human beings in His image, but we blew our

relationship with God and were sent away from our garden home. But we have not been sent away from God's love. To save us from our sin, God promised to send His Son as our Savior.

God shared His salvation plan with Abraham and his descendants. He asked them to perform sacrifice rituals to anticipate Christ's saving work. His promise of a Savior was sewn throughout the tapestry of the Israelites' history.

When the time was right, God sent His Son, Jesus Christ, to be our Redeemer. Jesus shared God's message of salvation through quiet talks with His disciples and mighty sermons to thousands. He spoke with authority, and demonstrated His authority by many powerful miracles.

But Jesus' main task was to be the perfect sacrifice for the sins of all humankind. He knew why the Father sent Him, and Christ shared Him with us. The amazing thing is that Jesus completed the lesson plan that black Friday. He loves us and willingly suffered all the indignities and agonies. His once-for-all sacrifice was complete in God's eyes. On Easter morning, the validity of God's plan was evident.

Jesus commissioned His followers, including us, to share His salvation message with all people. We are sent. Let's share!

Prayer:
Just as I am; Thy love unknown
Has broken ev'ry barrier down;
Now to be Thine, yea, Thine alone,
O Lamb of God, I come, I come.
(*Lutheran Worship* 359:6)

Homework:
Share God's salvation story with someone besides your students. Let that person see how important it is to you.

Golden Calves

Reading: Exodus 20:3

You shall have no other gods before Me.

Sports, movie stars, money, television, good looks, music, food or drink, peers, self-gratification . . .
Do you ever find yourself, or your students, worshiping these modern golden calves?

Our students are not blind and deaf to the influences around them. Inappropriate messages blast at them from magazines, movies, TV shows, music, and billboards. Kids are bombarded with "you gotta have" and "it only costs" until they are numb.

And what about us? Our golden calves might include things-to-get-done lists, lessons to prepare, meetings to attend, and sleep.

Items like these become idols when they become all-consuming tasks in our lives. We have so much to do that we may begin skipping Bible study and prayer. Though we teach God's Word, our personal Bible may get dusty while our prayer life gets rusty.

Thank God, He's God! He forgave the Israelites' idol worship and He will forgive ours also, because of Christ's redeeming work. This grace gives us total forgiveness. Gratitude for this forgiveness leads us to God's altar for worship and praise, and His Holy Spirit motivates our sanctified life. It is His continuing work in our lives that prevents busy-ness from turning into idol-ness.

Prayer:
Jehovah, let me now adore You,
For where, Lord, is there such a God as You?
With joyful songs I come before You;
Oh, let Your Spirit teach my heart anew
To praise You in His name through whom alone
Our songs can please You through Your blessed Son!
(*Lutheran Worship* 446:1)

Homework:
Take a personal, occupational, and spiritual inventory.
Pray about the things that keep you from spending personal time with God.

Hope

Reading: Romans 12:12

Be joyful in hope, patient in affliction, faithful in prayer.

As I stepped out on the front porch, I heard a sudden burst of fluttering wings, and a bird flew away, startling me.

"What in the world?" I gasped.

Looking around, I found a nest in the hanging basket directly in front of our door and mailbox. Later, my son heard cooing and we realized a pair of mourning doves had taken up residence there. A few days later two tiny eggs appeared in the nest, and we knew we had to take action.

My husband roped off the porch and put up a temporary mailbox to keep people from bothering the new mother. We named her Hope and cautiously joined in the baby watch.

Hope sat on the eggs patiently and calmly for a couple weeks. But she was ever watchful, and one of her brown eyes followed us closely if we got too close. We all celebrated when the two baby doves hatched!

Now we watched the babies develop and grow feathers. When would they fly away? It took a while for Hope to convince them they were ready, but finally the young birds spread their wings and took off. What a lesson in patience and trust we learned!

Your classroom is something like a nest for fledgling flyers. How is your patient waiting for progress holding out?

Students don't "hatch" quickly, but God's gift of patience will help you nurture your students during the growing process. Some students will gain their wings quickly and soar beyond you. Others will need a gentle prod, but then they, too, will take off. Of course, a few students may need to be shoved out of the nest, but do it in love, certain that they are ready for the challenge.

Read again Romans 12:12. "Be joyful in hope, patient in affliction, faithful in prayer."

Yes, your fledglings will one day leave you. That's a reason to celebrate. Until then, be watchful—and teach your students to be watchful for the devil's wiles. Help them learn to rely on God for protection and forgiveness, just as you do.

The God who gently pushed you out of the nest years ago

will refill your "nest" each year with students who need your assurance that they can fly.

Prayer:

Dear God, I can learn much from Your creation. Make me observant so I pass these lessons on to my students. It isn't enough to teach science without pointing out Your providential hand working in the world. In Jesus' grace-filled name. Amen.

Homework:

Look around today. What lesson from nature can you and your class learn?

Promotion Sunday

Reading: John 9:4

As long as it is day, we must do the work of Him who sent Me. Night is coming, when no one can work.

It was promotion Sunday at church, and our Sunday school superintendent rushed back and forth. He seemed to be mumbling to himself. I heard, "So many children and so little time!" He reminded me of the white rabbit in *Alice in Wonderland.* I chuckled softly and then stepped closer to offer my assistance. Gratefully, he assigned me some items from his list and we both scurried.

Later, as the students received their awards, I watched the superintendent again. He loved these children and prayed for their eternal salvation. But I also knew he prayed for all the ones who didn't attend regularly. He felt the shortness of time God gives each of us to work for His kingdom, and he tried every week to reach as many children as he could.

Reaching children and parents who don't know Jesus is the major task of a teacher's life, and a major responsibility. God works through His Word and Sacraments. The Holy Spirit works faith in the Savior. But who is to plant and water the seed? We, the teachers, are tools God uses to build His church.

We teach while serving as pastors, secretaries, bus drivers, doctors, nurses, homemakers, or in any occupation. Jesus has told us to make disciples by baptizing and "teaching them to obey everything I have commanded you" (Matthew 28:20). It's not a suggestion or a request. It's a command!

Who knows? You may be the one teaching tool God is using right now to reach a certain child. The first credential you need is the desire to bring little ones to the Lord.

It can sound daunting, yes, but Jesus also said, "And surely I am with you always, to the very end of the age" (Matthew 28:20). With a coach like that, we can all be successful teachers!

Step right up and accept your promotion. God has chosen you to be one of His teachers. Time is flying by, and there are so many children.

Prayer:
Dear Teacher of us all, I quake sometimes when I ponder the responsibility you have placed before me. Help me share the love of Jesus with the students You put before me. Keep my lessons fresh and pointing to You. Amen.

Homework:
Think of how you got started teaching for Jesus. Identify an adult or young person with teaching potential. Ask God's help and then approach that individual to talk about teaching.

A Praise Parade

Reading: Psalm 100:1–2

Shout for joy to the Lord, all the earth. Worship the Lord with gladness; come before Him with joyful songs.

Rose Bowl. Independence Day. Mardi Gras. Chinese New Year. No matter what the occasion, I love parades!

Children love parades too. In fact, if given the chance, they'll work for hours preparing for their own parade. Their enthusiasm and originality will be boundless!

I challenged my class to present a parade of praise for the surrounding neighborhood. After the happy shouts died down, the children divided into committees to make preparations.

One group devised a variety of eye-catching items to carry— balloons, streamers, pennants, and a large banner to lead the group. The banner proclaimed our purpose in bold bright letters: A Parade of Praise to God. You couldn't miss it!

The second group looked through songbooks to choose songs with messages of God's love and forgiveness for all. The rest of us were soon humming and singing along with them.

The next group wanted to "shout for joy to the Lord," so they reworded several sports cheers to celebrate God's grace. Then they wrote several originals. Fitting the words and beat together proved challenging, but the rehearsals were great fun.

The final group was in charge of our Gospel armor—something for us to wear. After much discussion, they decided on sandwich-boards with a cross on the front and a crown on the back. They also wrote Revelation 2:10 on each sandwich-board: "Be faithful, even to the point of death, and I will give you the crown of life."

At last the day arrived. We marched down the sidewalk, singing a song to share our faith. The neighbors we passed were first amazed, but then smiled in appreciation. Some even told us, "God loves you too!"

The kids and I learned that witnessing doesn't have to be scary, preparation is required, and God opens people's hearts to His message. Praise Him forever!

Prayer:
Praise God, from whom all blessings flow;
Praise Him, all creatures here below;
Praise Him above, O heavenly host;
Praise Father, Son, and Holy Ghost.

Homework:
Plan a new way for your students to witness their faith.
Be original! How about organizing a bake sale and giving out student-made Gospel tracts with purchases?

Storms!

Reading: Psalm 23:1

The Lord is my shepherd, I shall not be in want.

Trying to be as calm as possible, I gave the instructions for the tornado warning. The class had been overexcited with the lightning and thunder anyway, but now the lid blew off. Some cheered the break in the routine; some tried to be calm; and some turned white and tearful with fear.

I wasn't much better, as I was raised to have a very healthy respect for these powerful and unpredictable storms. But I shepherded my charges to the church basement as quickly as possible. I made sure everyone sat in the heads-covered position. Then we began our charged-up waiting period.

Suddenly, a small voice in the middle of my group started, "The Lord is my shepherd, I shall not be in want." One by one, her classmates picked it up. You see, that psalm had been our memory assignment the last few Sundays, and we had learned that King David trusted God to take care of him in any adversity.

As I joined Lisa and the rest, I looked around and realized that older students and their teachers had joined us in reciting the psalm. The younger students were quietly listening and being comforted too.

When we reached "Even though I walk through the valley of the shadow of death, I will fear no evil," we were not speaking a tentative prayer. It was a confident statement of faith. We *knew* God was with us.

While we waited out the storm, we sang songs of peace and joy and eternal hope. Finally, the all clear was sounded, and we returned to our classrooms.

Several children thanked Lisa for starting the psalm, and we all thanked God for His protection.

"Now where were we, class?" I began, and Jason said, "In God's hands."

Prayer:

Dear Protector, I cannot possibly know all of the times You have kept me from harm, but I do know You're here with me at all times. Thank You for Your constant care for me and my students. Help me always to be a healthy example of confident faith when sudden danger occurs. We are all in Your hands. Amen.

Homework:

Cut weather maps out of the newspaper for a few days and study them. Thank God for the power and protection He showers on His people.

God's Needling

Reading: Psalm 52:8–9

But I am like an olive tree flourishing in the house of God; I trust in God's unfailing love for ever and ever. I will praise You forever for what You have done; in Your name I will hope, for Your name is good. I will praise You in the presence of Your saints.

A wise friend once said, "If we stop learning, we stop living." That's especially true for Christian teachers. Lessons can be learned everywhere, if we only pay attention. God has even spoken to me through the pages of my counted cross-stitch pattern books.

When you are stitching pictures or sayings out of hundreds of tiny x's, you have a lot of time to reflect on each one. I did a piece about a strong marriage, and I thanked God for my 22 years of love and blessings with my own husband. I've done wall hangings about little ones, and my heart rejoiced in my two children. Finding appropriate sayings for their teachers challenges me each year. I still think about the one that said, "The greatest aid to adult education is children." How true!

Two stitching projects have stayed with me the longest, rather like an echo God sends through my mind from time to time. The first one said, "When God closes a door, He opens a window." I made it for some friends who were retiring, but it has resounded often in my mind, especially when I've tried new types of writing ministry.

The second project brought me up short with the saying, "Let Go and Let God." Wow! How many times I had run off on my own to attempt to solve a problem. It simply doesn't work well. But when I turn my dilemma over to God, He straightens me out and leads me the way He wants me to go. You'd think I'd learn!

Thank God that He hasn't given up on me, and He continues to forgive my willfulness. He has lessons yet for me to learn, and more directions to follow. Where are we going next, Lord?

Prayer:
Jesus, still lead on
Till our rest be won;
Heav'nly leader, still direct us,
Still support, console, protect us,
Till we safely stand
In our fatherland. Amen.
(*Lutheran Worship* 386:4)

Homework:
Think through your daily activities. Are you watching for lessons from God? He will teach you today.

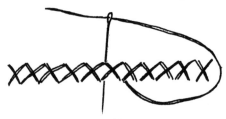

Attitudes

Reading: Matthew 21:28–31

"What do you think? There was a man who had two sons. He went to the first and said, 'Son, go and work today in the vineyard.' 'I will not,' he answered, but later he changed his mind and went. Then the father went to the other son and said the same thing. He answered, 'I will, sir,' but he did not go. Which of the two did what his father wanted?" "The first," they answered.

Rena bounced into the classroom one morning wearing a bright yellow T-shirt. Across the front, in big blue letters, were the words "I have an attitude." As she danced around the room greeting her friends, I wondered about it. Her outgoing personality didn't seem to fit the shirt's message. When I lightly asked her about it, her face clouded for an instant.

"I don't know what it means. My mom got it for me," Rena said. Then she merrily went her way; but the Rena I knew didn't fit the T-shirt.

The two sons in our Bible reading also had an attitude. The first one challenged his father with an out-and-out refusal to obey. His stubbornness was obvious, but then he repented and did as his father had asked. The second son was hypocritical. At first he agreed to do what his father said, but then he ignored the order. His stubbornness wasn't as forthright, but it was still there. Stubbornness is the student attitude that I find the most difficult to deal with. It interferes with the relationship I try to build with students. When they get that "I-don't-care-what-you-say" look, it's very exasperating. How to reach them?

Thank God, He knows how to break down rocky defenses—with love. It's the only thing that will break through a child's emotional fortress. A student responds to loving forgiveness from a teacher, and from God. Love—motivated by the love God has for us—is the strongest way to reach people. That kind of love is patient and kind. "It does not envy, it does not boast, it is not proud. It is not rude, it is not self-seeking, it is not easily angered, it keeps no record of wrongs" (1 Corinthians 13:4–5).

So how's your attitude? God loves you, no matter what your T-shirt says.

Dear Father, prod me to seek out my students from behind their attitudes. Turn my own stubbornness into a constant love for You and Your children. When I'm confronted with a willful student, help me hold my temper in check. Let that student see You in me. Through Him who is Love personified. Amen.

Homework:

Pick out a student who's hard to love and concentrate your attention in that child's direction. Don't give up! He or she may not be used to receiving love from a teacher.

P & D

Reading: Hebrews 2:14–17

Since the children have flesh and blood, He too shared in their humanity so that by His death He might destroy him who holds the power of death—that is, the devil—and free those who all their lives were held in slavery by their fear of death. For surely it is not angels He helps, but Abraham's descendants. For this reason He had to be made like His brothers in every way, in order that He might become a merciful and faithful high priest in service to God, and that He might make atonement for the sins of the people.

It always happens in February. Valentine's Day is past and Easter seems to be eons away. The sun doesn't stay out long enough, and the weather can be depressing.

What is this "it"? "It" goes under several names: the blahs, winter doldrums, or cabin fever. But whatever you label it, the phenomenon is real, and it hits teachers and students alike. How to combat it?

A few years ago, I read about a motivational tool called P & D, and I decided to try it. P & D stands for *pride and diligence.* You encourage your students to do their best work by awarding P & D's as well as grades. If an assignment is well done in all aspects, you put a big P & D on the paper along with the grade.

Using the P & D system perks me up and encourages me to look for excellence, not just completion. I also find that my teaching moves up a notch because the technique challenges me as well as the students. If I expect my students to do well, then, with God's help, I must improve too.

God gave us the epitome of a P & D about 2,000 years ago— His Son to be our Savior. When we were mired in the doldrums of sin, darker than any February day, Jesus came for us.

God the Father did the P part when He sent His only Son. To paraphrase a familiar saying, the Father cared enough to send the very best. He sent the only one who could accomplish our salvation: the God-man, Jesus Christ.

Jesus added the D part as He lived a perfect life all the way to the cross. He did it out of love for us. His perfect love led Him through His dusty, impoverished life to a cruel, pain-wracked death. But He did all that God required, so we could be forgiven. We can once again approach the Father's throne, secure in our God-won P & D.

Prayer:
Dear Jesus Christ, it amazes me every time I realize how much You love me. Keep me grateful for Your immense love that led You to sacrifice Yourself on the cross so that I can live. Please bring my students to a stronger faith in You. May they, too, celebrate Your grace eternally. I pray with faith in your sacrifice. Amen.

Homework:
Think of a very dear person in your life. Could you purposely give that person up to a painful death? God did that for you.

I Dare You!

Reading: Psalm 119:174–75

I long for Your salvation, O Lord, and Your law is my delight.
Let me live that I may praise You, and may Your laws sustain
me.

"I dare you!" These three words put me in some pretty precarious positions as a child. Older children, and my brothers, discovered I couldn't ignore their outrageous suggestions, and they egged me on.

I climbed in trees higher than was safe, and then had to have help getting back down. Playing "chicken" on our bikes led to several accidents. My guardian angel must have been a basket case!

The Holy Spirit gives us the ultimate dare when He calls us to be Christians. He dares us to be different from those around us, something like a penguin who dares to wear a red bow tie.

We live as forgiven sinners, saints who recognize Christ's redeeming work in us. God's Holy Spirit helps us restrain sinful desires and follow God's commandments. We use Christian principles in our dealings with people. And we share our faith with our children. But do we really stand out as different from those around us? How proud are we of our red bow ties?

Our Scripture reading talks of praising and singing, not cursing or swearing. It calls us to ask for God's help in understanding situations. Do we look for His hand at work—or do we chalk things up to fate? When problems arise, do we turn to God as our greatest resource, or our last resort? In other words, do we try to blend in with the crowd? Do we only wear our red bow ties to Christian gatherings?

As Christian teachers, we live under a magnifying glass. Our students may be amazed to see us in the grocery store—not realizing we eat food like other mortals. They're curious to see how we act there. If they could follow us around, what would they discover? Would they see us shed the Christian skins we wear in class?

God calls us to be living, breathing examples of how His children live in everyday life. Put on your blood-red bow tie and wear it with pride. God loves you. He dares you, and backs you with the power of His Spirit, to live your faith among those He has placed around you.

Prayer:

Lord, give me the full power of Your Holy Spirit so that my faith in You shines in my life and makes a difference in my relationships with the people around me. In Jesus' name. Amen.

Homework:

Wear a piece of Christian jewelry today. Use it as an opportunity to talk about God's love for you.

Bible Helps

Reading: 2 Timothy 3:16

All Scripture is God-breathed and is useful for teaching, rebuking, correcting and training in righteousness.

The fourth graders in my day school class were trying to get the times tables down really well before we went on to longer multiplication and division. We had played games, done oral and written drills, and used every other learning tool I could devise. Then one day a new idea came to me. Why not?

Some eyebrows went up the next day when I told the children to get out their Bibles during math class.

"What?" Jared said. "It's not religion time." But the children got them out, skeptics though they were. I challenged the kids to find biblical images for the numerals 1–12. We proceeded to search our Bibles for numbers and came up with:

1 Savior
2 of each animal on the ark
3 persons of the Trinity
4 gospels
5 loaves of bread with the two fish
6 days of creation
7 days of Holy Week
8 people saved from the flood
9 for NINEveh
10 commandments
11 disciples remained faithful
12 tribes of Israel

Then we were ready for the next step.

"Okay, Jared, what are five loaves times four gospels?"

This time his eyebrows just about left his head, but he answered correctly.

"How about ten commandments times twelve tribes?" As I continued the children were delighted with the game. They started making up problems for each other, and time ran out before their enthusiasm did. They wanted to do Bible numbers over and over. Some challenged classmates by finding different references for the numerals.

God entered our lesson and extended it. He invited His children into His Word. They searched at school, and then took the task home and got their parents involved. While parents and children searched the Word for a math game, they couldn't help reviewing again God's wonderful plan for our salvation and His great love for us. The Holy Spirit built up His church.

The final word on the subject came from Jared. "God's Word does help us with everything."

Prayer:

Dear God, who numbers the hairs on my head, keep me in Your Word. Lead me to set aside time each day, individually and with groups, to study Your will for Your people. Help me push aside distractions so I can truly say, "Speak, Lord. Your servant is listening." Amen.

Homework:

Does this compute? $1 \times 10{,}000 = 0$. Yes, it does, when we say 1 Savior's death and resurrection $\times$ my thousands of sins = nothing left of my guilt. Praise the Lord daily for His marvelous multiplication.

Mr. Nobody

Reading: 1 John 1:8–9

If we claim to be without sin, we deceive ourselves and the truth is not in us. If we confess our sins, He is faithful and just and will forgive us our sins and purify us from all unrighteousness.

I always have one more student than desks. This extra student is hard to find because he's invisible, but he is, nonetheless, there.

He's the student who drops the paper towels all over the restroom floor. He's the one who makes pencil marks in books. He leaves the ball on the playground. He does all these things and more, because no one else in my class does them.

I call him Mr. Nobody. He must be real. When no other student admits to causing messes or difficulties, then Mr. Nobody must be around. He moves around a lot, but his favorite place seems to be standing right behind other students, bothering them.

Do you recognize this tongue-in-cheek picture of the "I-didn't-do-it" syndrome that runs through all classes? I think Mr. Nobody is a constant presence because students learn to avoid blame at all costs. Sadly, many students don't see their parents admit their wrongs and ask for forgiveness.

How do we teach confession, both to God and to each other? Lecturing about sin won't do it. Children have to experience confession and forgiveness, and it starts with the teacher. When we confess our sins of anger or impatience to God and our students, and ask their forgiveness, it's an eye-opener.

God doesn't force us to confess, but His Spirit continues to work in us, bringing us to repentance. And God's forgiveness is instantaneous and complete. That's our example for forgiving our students: complete forgiveness, no strings attached.

Let your classroom be a laboratory for experiencing God's grace and forgiveness. As you set an example in freely forgiving students, they will follow suit.

When the day comes that an especially recalcitrant student mumbles an apology—without prompting from you—rejoice!

Prayer:
Savior, I admit that I don't always confess my sins against my students. Prod me to do so, to You and to them, so they learn that confession and forgiveness are integral to Christian living. In Your forgiving name. Amen.

Homework:
Write acrostics for CONFESS and FORGIVE, using instances when you and your students especially need forgiveness. Place your acrostics in an obvious place as a reminder to yourself.

Again!

Reading: Proverbs 15:1

A gentle answer turns away wrath, but a harsh word stirs up anger.

God, please help me, I prayed silently. I am so tired of this boy.

For the sixth time during the lesson, Sean had blurted out an answer or unnecessary comment.

Positive reinforcement be hanged, I thought, my patience spent. I'm ready to send him out of the room, just for some peace.

My students challenge me regularly with their intense, enthusiastic curiosity. But Sean was even more challenging. He had been diagnosed as an ADD child. ADD abbreviates Attention Deficit Disorder and means Sean has trouble blocking out any surrounding activity.

But knowing about his problem doesn't make it any easier to handle, I complained to myself. Why doesn't he ever miss a Sunday?

The Sunday school superintendent tapped at the door. "Mrs. Loontjer, could you please let Sean come to the office for an important phone call?"

"Of course," I answered, silently blessing whoever was calling.

All too soon, Sean was back with a shout, "My baby was born!" The phone call from his father had announced the arrival of seven-and-a-half pound Patrick Ian O'Brien, a new brother.

I almost missed the tension in Sean's eyes and proceeded with the lesson, but God forced me to look again. Sean's attention was *VERY* focused now—on me and my reaction.

"Can you tell us more about Patrick?" I heard myself ask, and it was right. The lesson could wait for a moment. Let him talk, my heart advised. Sean poured out his information, and the rest of our class time passed calmly.

There were more Sundays to endure with Sean and his behavior, but we would make it. Thanks, God, for answering my frustrated plea. And keep answering it, please?

Dear patient Teacher in heaven, how often You must shake Your head in frustration as You watch me muddy up Your message with my blunders. I can never attain Your perfect patience, but give me a small measure each day, to help me learn from all my Seans. In Your name I pray, again. Amen.

Homework:

Think back to a very challenging student you've had and try to find out what he or she is doing now. Write a note of Christian encouragement to that person.

Harold and Esther

Reading: Psalm 71:17–18

Since my youth, O God, You have taught me, and to this day I declare Your marvelous deeds. Even when I am old and gray, do not forsake me, O God, till I declare Your power to the next generation, Your might to all who are to come.

An old TV commercial came to mind: How do you spell relief? Jokingly, I said to myself, R-E-T-I-R-E-M-E-N-T. Yes, it had been one of those weeks and I was washed out. But then the faces of two people popped into my mind's eye. Harold and Esther had been teachers for a total of 75 years and were now retired. They must have had a lot of washed-out evenings!

Harold and Esther served in their congregation seven days a week, teaching and doing whatever else was needed. There was no such thing as specialization in those days. If they were asked to teach Sunday school or coordinate the children's Christmas service, they did their best, following God's direction.

When Harold married Esther, God gave him more than a wife. She was a helpmeet, coworker, and soul mate. God truly is the third person in their relationship. God touched hundreds of students and their parents through Harold and Esther. His kingdom grew through their work. Just about everyone in their congregation can tell a Harold-and-Esther story that will make you smile and shake your head.

Compared to Harold and Esther, I am a toddler in God's service. Can I learn from their example in following God's lead?

Pastor wants me to start a women's Bible study group. Can I do that? The high school youth Bible study group is so large that they need another teacher. Can I do that? How about children's lessons during worship services? Could I lead them?

I hear You, God. So now, how do you spell relief? C-O-M-M-I-T-M-E-N-T to God, and R-E-L-I-A-N-C-E on His Spirit's leading.

Prayer:
Dear Lord, I thank You for Your gift of faithful servants in the church. They have given You their whole-hearted service for many years. Give me a greater measure of commitment to You and to my students. Lead me into service that will further Your kingdom. Through Jesus. Amen.

Homework:
Think back to a teacher or pastor who influenced your life. Write a note to thank that person and share some experiences from your ministry.

God's Environment

Reading: Genesis 1:28

God blessed them and said to them, "Be fruitful and increase in number; fill the earth and subdue it. Rule over the fish of the sea and the birds of the air and over every living creature that moves on the ground."

Pollutants. Recycle. Landfills. Nuclear waste. Environment. Even young children are aware of these watchwords of our society. Finally we are facing up to the environmental depletion that scientists have been warning about for years. How did we get into this mess?

God certainly didn't put the first humans into a life-threatening environment. When He finished creating our world, "God saw all that He had made, and it was very good" (Genesis 1:31). He created a perfect life-sustaining environment for His people. Everything in nature was in perfect balance and ran according to the laws God had ordained. So what happened?

Sin happened. Satan was the world's original polluter. And Adam and Eve joined him when they capitulated to his temptations. The beauty was soiled and our environment became hostile.

We have twisted God's instructions to "fill the earth and subdue it" (Genesis 1:28). Again and again, we have used these words to justify our greed, whether in a conscious manner or not. "What's in it for me?" has been our environmental slogan.

As Christian teachers we have the opportunity and the responsibility to influence our students' environmental behavior. Thanks to God's forgiveness through Jesus, our pollution of sin is removed. God leads us to use our blessings to be a blessing to others and care for the world He created for us.

In environmental terms, we foster a loving place where children can see how recycling God's love makes their individual worlds stronger and safer. Then we lead them to look around and see what they can do to improve and preserve their physical environment.

God's forgiveness in Christ impacts our world through us by cleaning up sin's pollution. Let's pray we, and our students, will have an environmental impact.

Prayer:

Creator of all, thank You for awakening me to my world's sorry condition. I pray that it's not too late for change. Forgive me for my greedy and callous behavior. Keep me mindful of environmental problems and of how my students and I can help prepare people to enter Your new heaven and earth through faith in Christ. In the name of Jesus. Amen.

Homework:

Today, alone or with your students, begin a new project to help preserve the environment.

Power of the Cross

Reading: 1 Corinthians 1:17–18

For Christ did not send me to baptize, but to preach the gospel—not with words of human wisdom, lest the cross of Christ be emptied of its power. For the message of the cross is foolishness to those who are perishing, but to us who are being saved it is the power of God.

"Are your kids learning about the power of the cross on the late, late show?" These words on a poster shocked me. The picture showed a vampire about to bite a woman's neck, and in the background was the shadow of a hand holding the cross!

How does the world view the cross?

Often the media presents a derisive depiction of Christians, and of Christ Himself. The jewelry industry makes thousands of dollars each year on the sale of Christian items. How many people, wearing a piece of Christian jewelry, stand ready to witness their faith in Christ? In Arlington National Cemetery, crosses are used as grave markers. It's impressive to see the continuous rows of crosses, but did each of the service people buried there know Christ as their Savior?

St. Paul knew about outside influences that defame the Good News of Christ's crucifixion and resurrection. "For the message of the cross is foolishness to those who are perishing, but to us who are being saved it is the power of God."

Do we and our students lead double lives at times? Do we profess our faith openly and confidently at Sunday school, and then go home and hide our faith so we don't seem foolish to our peers?

We know the price God was charged for our eternal souls, and we live in gratitude for His paid-in-full receipt. Paul states our teaching mission boldly: "For Christ did not send me to baptize, but to preach the gospel—not with words of human wisdom, lest the cross of Christ be emptied of its power" (1 Corinthians 1:17).

Pray that God will make us bold to proclaim the Good News of what Christ has done for us on the cross. Our students watch us to see how the power of the cross rules our lives. Let's pray that they may see redeemed Christians who are wise in the knowledge of all that God has done for us.

Prayer:

Dear Savior, You earned my salvation and never failed to express love and forgiveness in Your daily life. Assist my students and me as we grow in God's grace. Let us proclaim Your Good News in our words and actions. In Your name. Amen.

Homework:

Help your students note different uses of the symbol of the cross. Pray together that you may make a bold witness of Christ crucified.

Tara's Lesson

Reading: Luke 19:17

"Well done, my good servant!" his master replied. "Because you have been trustworthy in a very small matter, take charge of ten cities."

Roses are red.
Violets are blue.
I want to be
A teacher like you.

It made my day! This simple little poem appeared on my desk in the center of a hand-illustrated picture of a chalkboard. The chalkboard was filled with math problems and spelling words.

But Tara's poem was in the center, with a large purple cross directly above it.

Tara was in fourth grade that year, an exuberant, Scandinavian blond. She loved soccer, her baby brother, and school—in that order. She had announced early in the year that she was going to be a teacher, and I guess I hadn't done anything to put her off. She liked to play school during indoor recess, and many times I would chuckle to hear my own phrasings and intonations. Other times I would cringe to hear my impatient phrases echoed.

I thought about Tara again later that day, and I realized God had placed her in my class as an example of childlike faith. She loved to discuss Bible stories and never failed to learn her memory work. But, much more than that, she loved her Lord Jesus and she lived her love.

Tara was kind to people without expecting something in return. She gave encouragement and helped others when they asked, but she didn't push herself on a friend. She begged to help me with some of my tasks each day. The clincher, though, was Tara's total forgiveness. When a problem occurred with a friend, Tara willingly forgave AND forgot the incident. She followed the example of Jesus, who had first loved her.

Looking at Tara's picture, I found myself saying:

Roses are red.
Violets are blue.
I want to be
A Christian like you.

Prayer:
Thank You, Jesus, for the children You put in my class. They are my refreshers, for they reflect You. Strengthen their faith as they grow physically, and let them dedicate their lives to Your service. Help my own faith grow too. In Your blessed name. Amen.

Homework:
Write a short poem or prayer of thanks to God for the "little Christs" you teach.

Tongue in Check

Reading: James 3:9–10

With the tongue we praise our Lord and Father, and with it we curse men, who have been made in God's likeness. Out of the same mouth come praise and cursing. My brothers, this should not be.

"Teacher, I know the answer. It's on the tip of my tongue, but it won't come out!" John explained.

Consider the tongue. It's a small muscle used in chewing and speaking, but, oh, the damage it can cause! We have several clichés referring to this part of the anatomy: Bite your tongue. Keep a civil tongue in your head. Give him a tongue-lashing. She's tongue-tied. The cat's got his tongue.

Notice that there isn't a positive one in the bunch. People know how hurtful this muscle can be. God knows, too, and dedicated an entire chapter of the Bible (James 3) to the tongue.

What does all this talk about the tongue have to do with teachers? Everything! We are in the communication business, and our "audience" tunes in to all our methods. Kids watch our faces and our body language. Our expression can easily cancel what our lips are saying.

Take a look at the strong contrast found in Proverbs 12:18. "Reckless words pierce like a sword, but the tongue of the wise brings healing." Too often we use "reckless words" without thinking them through first.

Pray for a "tongue of the wise" to promote healing. So many of our students need to hear healing words. Proverbs 15:1 tells us, "A gentle answer turns away wrath, but a harsh word stirs up anger." Gentle answers are so necessary because children get enough harsh words from others in their lives. They long for gentle answers from the teachers who show them Jesus' love.

Speak God's name in love. Sing His name in joy. Pray His name in reverence. Shout His name in praise!

Prayer:
Jesus, You gave Your disciples the words to say when talking to Your Father. I pray today that You would make me think carefully about what I say to my students. Control my tongue. Let me use it as a tool to

witness Your love. May I always be prepared to speak words of forgiveness. In Your name. Amen.

Homework:

Memorize the words of Psalm 19:14: "May the words of my mouth and the meditation of my heart be pleasing in Your sight, O Lord, my Rock and my Redeemer."

Going to a New School

Reading: Genesis 12:1

The Lord had said to Abram, "Leave your country, your people and your father's household and go to the land I will show you."

THE call had come! My husband and I had turned down other job offers before this. God had led us to believe that He wanted us where we were. But now He was leading us to accept new teaching positions in a city a thousand miles away.

Besides all of the obvious stresses of packing and moving, we were anxious over other things as well. We had served as Christian day school teachers in our congregation for 18 years. The move meant leaving many good things. That was an emotional issue.

We were accepting a sizable cut in pay. That was a fiscal issue. And, in effect, we were starting our careers over. We had to reestablish our reputations as effective teachers in the classroom and as capable leaders in the church. This, then, was a professional issue.

How did Abraham do it? God didn't give him any road maps or itineraries. God didn't even give him a final destination. He just said, "Go!" and Abraham didn't question it.

My husband and I knew the answer. Abraham did it by faith. God directed him to leave his home of many years "and go to the land I will show you." Abraham accepted God's call, packed his family and flocks, and followed the Lord's leadership.

Now it was our turn to leave home and follow God's guidance. If Abraham and Sarah could do it in ancient times, with all their camels and sheep, we surely could do it in modern times.

So like Abraham, trusting in God's guidance and direction, we turned our faces—and vehicles—west. God would show us the plan for our service to Him in the new place.

Prayer:
Dear Leader, I thank You today for Your continual presence in my life. Help me always to see my personal pillar of cloud as You lead me from place to place. Keep my eyes on You so that my path won't wander from Your will. In Jesus' name. Amen.

Homework:
Get out a road map and trace the path on which God has led you in your service to Him. Thank Him for His constant guidance.

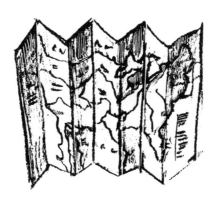

Blinders for the Lord

Reading: Isaiah 64:4

Since ancient times no one has heard, no ear has perceived, no eye has seen any God besides You, who acts on behalf of those who wait for Him.

I was amazed when I read in the newspaper that city children think that milk, bread, and eggs come "from the store." I took it upon myself to make sure my Sunday school class wouldn't be so uninformed. I found an old-fashioned farm close to our church and made arrangements for a field trip.

The first thing my class had to learn was that animals don't like to be charged at or chased. Jerry learned the hard way when a gaggle of geese turned the tables and started chasing him.

Everyone had to comment on the farm smell, of course. Teresa spent the entire tour breathing through her mouth!

As we proceeded, the children's eyes were opened to the marvels of farm life. They loved to feel the baby chicks' softness and the baby calf's sucking on their fingers. A few brave souls reached into a hen's nest and discovered eggs. But they learned the most from watching the plow horses.

These horses are gentle giants, and the students were awed by their size. As the farmer guided the plow behind his team, all kinds of questions popped out of the students' mouths. I noticed Andy was staring carefully at the horses' heads. Finally he asked, "What are those leather things by their eyes?"

I explained that blinders prevent the horses from being distracted. The blinders keep them looking straight ahead and going in the direction the farmer desires.

Andy digested this information and then said, "Too bad God doesn't put those on people. Then they wouldn't get off the road to heaven."

Yes, there are dozens of distractions and temptations that we must avoid each day. But God will steer us clear of them if we keep our eyes firmly focused on the cross. Oh, for insight like Andy's!

Prayer

Dear God and Father, please give me a childlike faith so I can see Your hand in all that surrounds me. When I'm tempted to stray from the course You've set for me, gently guide me back and forgive my waywardness. In Your Son's name. Amen.

Homework:

Identify the distractions that can prevent you from walking in God's way. Pray for divine blinders and the Spirit's help in keeping your eyes on Christ's cross.

Sarah's Song

Reading: Romans 5:8

But God demonstrates His own love for us in this: While we were still sinners, Christ died for us.

"X-X-X marks the spot," Sarah was singing, and I smiled at her jubilation as I prepared for another day of teaching. With all I was doing, it took me a while to tune in to the next line of her song: "I guess I'm not doing too hot." I looked up quickly and realized she was singing about her returned assignment papers. Oh, no!

When I first began teaching, I used X's to mark incorrect answers on papers. Those X's were the only marks I made on the papers, except to note the grade.

Now I was brought up short by a little girl whose self-image was draining away. Every red X on her papers was a blow to her confidence, when she should have been enjoying success.

I made a quick note on my things-to-do list—"Sarah's song"—and then began class. As I taught, I began counting how many negative comments I made, and compared that to the number of positive statements. Wow! It was a shocking revelation.

That evening, in my private devotions, I talked to God about Sarah's song and my negative comments. I asked His forgiveness and asked for help. I was a Christian teacher, whose job is to communicate the positive message of Christ's death and resurrection!

Thankfully, Jesus paid for these sins of negativism as well as all my others. His forgiveness was instantaneous, and I began to feel God's guidance as the following days unfolded.

God first led me to a more experienced teacher whom I admired. She suggested that I make a cheery comment—even if it was just to say I liked the child's new haircut—on at least one of every student's papers each day. That helped.

I can't say I broke my bad habits overnight, but God is a continuously forgiving God. And children are very forgiving too. Over the years, God has helped me find all kinds of ways to pat a child on the back.

When the day finally arrived that Sarah charged up to my desk and exclaimed, "Mrs. Loontjer, I got a happy face on every paper," I knew my behavior had changed.

Prayer:

Prayer:
Dear Master Teacher, You bless me each year with a new batch of students to teach. Don't let me dwell on their faults. Help me teach as You did, with love flowing from Your actions as well as Your lips. Forgive me when I fail You and my class. In Your name. Amen.

Homework:
Tape record a lesson. Compare the number of negative comments you make to the positive ones. Ask God to show you ways to give positive support to your students.

Mistaken Identity

Reading: 1 John 1:8–9

If we claim to be without sin, we deceive ourselves and the truth is not in us. If we confess our sins, He is faithful and just and will forgive us our sins and purify us from all unrighteousness.

Glowing—that's the way I was feeling that afternoon. That's the way King Midas must have felt at the beginning also.

Everything in my life was going right, and I was flying high. My children had brought home wonderful report cards. My colleagues were congratulating me about the way a big project had worked out. My husband was proud of the way I'd lost all that weight.

The topper came when a Sunday school lesson I had planned worked out so well that my students couldn't wait for the next class period. Hearing "What are we going to learn today?" just made me glow a bit more.

You're probably expecting to read about a fall, and you're right. The thing that brought me up short was an innocent comment by Tracey. As she left Sunday school, I overheard her say, "Mrs. Loontjer is the best teacher I've ever had. She's perfect."

At first I smiled smugly. And then God played Tracey's comment back in my mind. Perfect? Hardly!

That was a soul-searching week, full of uncomfortable thoughts. I had been proud of my accomplishments, thinking I had done everything on my own. I realized painfully that my self-righteous attitude was pulling me away from God. He had given me so many blessings, and I was stepping into the spotlight by myself.

How to get back in right standing with God? It didn't depend on me. I fell to my knees before the cross. Jesus had taken my punishment, even for my sins of self-importance.

Who did I think I was? Jesus Christ had taken my load of sin onto His innocent nature. I certainly wasn't in any position to try to pass myself off as perfect. Wait a minute! Christ took on my sinful identity so that in Him, God *does* see me as perfect. That's definitely a case of mistaken identity—thanks be to God! Next, I began to write a lesson on giving God the credit for leading us in our successes.

Prayer:

Dear perfect Son of God, You alone are my salvation. When I'm tempted to accept accolades for myself, please remind me of the source of my blessings. Thank You for dying for my sins so I can live in Your service, pronounced innocent because of Your sacrifice. Amen.

Homework:

Look into your mirror and be honest with yourself. Do you see a pretty good person in your own right, or a person who succeeds only because of God's blessing and guidance?

Training or Teaching?

Reading: Matthew 19:13–14

Then little children were brought to Jesus for Him to place His hands on them and pray for them. But the disciples rebuked those who brought them. Jesus said, "Let the little children come to Me, and do not hinder them, for the kingdom of heaven belongs to such as these."

"Sit up! Roll over! Beg!" These commands popped into my head as I observed the teacher who had been assigned as my supervisor for my student teaching experience.

The teacher used a stimulus-response approach for classroom control. The students were to be quiet instantly when she snapped the lights off and on. "Get out your books" meant "Get them out, put them on your desk, and fold your hands on top. Do NOT open them until permitted." One little girl made the mistake of approaching THE TEACHER'S DESK without raising her hand first.

Yikes! Is this what I have to do also, I wondered, as a student teacher under her supervision? My mind and heart rebelled as I watched. There was no room for spontaneity and love, even at recess. How could I help lead children to Jesus in an atmosphere like this?

Over the weeks, as I was allowed more leeway in the classroom, I tried to change the atmosphere. The students seemed a bit wary about my openness and acceptance at first, but then they started opening up to me.

The face of one little boy still sticks with me 23 years later. A learning disability prevented him from keeping up with the others, and the teacher wasn't interested in working with him on a one-to-one basis.

One day I sat down with Jerry in the corner and gave him an individual spelling test, pronouncing the words very slowly. He screwed up his face and concentrated. He didn't get 100 percent, but he did get his first C in spelling that year. The smile of accomplishment on Jerry's face was a joy to behold.

We can become stumbling blocks to our students' faith if we never show them the happiness and acceptance Jesus gives them. Children can relate to Jesus' love if they are taught in a loving, joyful atmosphere. Those first and second graders taught me about the forgiving nature of children, and reminded me how important it is to share God's unconditional love.

Prayer:

Dear Jesus, who loves all children, forgive me for teaching rigidly, for sharing facts about You and not sharing Your love. Help me teach as You taught. Keep love shining from my eyes, and let me always be ready to forgive when my students make a mistake. In Your name. Amen.

Homework:

Think about your teaching style. Do you demand grudging obedience, or earn loving respect? Ask God's help in sharing the love and acceptance Christ has won for you.

Bearing Fruit

Reading: Galatians 5:22–23

But the fruit of the Spirit is love, joy, peace, patience, kindness, goodness, faithfulness, gentleness and self-control. Against such things there is no law.

Each class seems to have its own collective personality. One group may be full of joy and kindness, but lack self-control. The next group may be a peaceful, patient crew, but their joy seems to be muted.

My most recent class is a good example. Sally is full of love and patience, even though she comes from a broken home. Tim's gentleness and joy shone when his baby sister was born. Cal's patience isn't evident until he starts working on an art project. Then he takes great pains with his creation. Mandy is one of the gentlest souls I've ever known. David hides his love behind a rough exterior, but his feelings are close to the surface. Josie is a joyful, exuberant girl, full of hugs and compliments for others. Jerry is intense and hard on himself, but his goodness shines forth each week. Kelly is an excellent student. But more than that, she's a kind girl who's always ready to help. Rich's joy is barely hidden below the surface and jumps out frequently. I can readily see God's Spirit at work in this class, gifting these students with the fruit He has nurtured.

Thanks to the Spirit's leading, these kids know with a certainty that God walks with them as their Savior, Shepherd, Protector, and best Friend.

Now, I wonder what the next group God gives me will be like
. . .

Prayer:
Spirit, show me the fruit You nurture in the students in my class. Let me be Your tool in their growth process. And, while we're talking, could You please give me and them an extra measure of self-control? Through Jesus. Amen.

Homework:
Thank God for the special fruit of the Spirit that is evident in your students' lives. You can write notes to the children, thanking them for sharing their Spirit-given gifts with you.

Are You a Superstar?

Reading: Matthew 25:19–21

After a long time the master of those servants returned and settled accounts with them. The man who had received the five talents brought the other five. "Master" he said, "you entrusted me with five talents. See, I have gained five more." His master replied, "Well done, good and faithful servant! You have been faithful with a few things; I will put you in charge of many things. Come and share your master's happiness!"

Name someone you consider a superstar. Is it someone in sports, film, business? Did you base your decision on popular appeal or market value? Would you call yourself a superstar?

Just what exactly is a superstar? I would define a superstar as a person who uses the talent given to him or her by God. A superstar practices using that talent day after day until it is honed to a superior point. Even when this excellence is recognized, he or she continues to strive for top-notch performance, and this effort may earn success for many years.

What about Christian teachers? Are we superstars in our chosen endeavor?

We have recognized our talent for teaching and have been led by the Holy Spirit into service in God's church. How do we perfect our talent? Do we look for new ways to present our lessons, or rely on the way we did it before? Do we attend classes, seminars, and teachers' meetings to improve our skills? Do we make time for private devotions and Bible study?

We'll never receive the salaries or fame of those people whom the world recognizes as superstars, but we do reap rewards. We gain the respect and love of our students. Parents often recognize and appreciate the sacrifices we make. Our colleagues are proud to work with us, and our congregation sees us as assets to its ministry.

But the greatest reward will come when we face our Lord and He says, "Well done, good and faithful servant." What more could a superstar want?

Prayer:
Dear Jesus, You certainly are the Superstar, yet You are also the greatest Servant who has ever lived. Your

sacrificial death won for me eternal life. Forgive me when I long for earthly rewards and pity myself for long hours spent in Your service. Let me gladly perfect my teaching talents in Your service, knowing that Your approval is the highest reward. Amen.

Homework:

Read a book or magazine article that will help you strengthen your teaching of Christ's Gospel.

Stuffed to Overflowing

Reading: Matthew 1:21

She will give birth to a son, and you are to give Him the name Jesus, because He will save His people from their sins.

Oh, yes, stocking stuffers, I reminded myself as I wrote my Christmas shopping list. While I thought about possibilities for each of my children, I hummed along with the carol "O Little Town of Bethlehem," which was playing on the radio.

Abruptly I stopped my busy-ness, and my mind leaped to all the gifts I had already received. I wouldn't even be going through all this hustle and bustle called Christmas if God hadn't given His Son to pay the price for my sins. Now that's a gift!

So in my spiritual stocking I first gently and lovingly placed a manger with a tiny babe. In that tiny body was all the love God felt for me, lying in a cattle trough and wearing swaddling clothes. I marveled as I remembered 1 John 4:9: "This is how God showed his love among us: He sent His one and only Son into the world that we might live through Him."

My wonder at God's love exploded into fireworks of joy. I heard the powerful message of the angels as they split the night sky with their glorious anthem of praise, "Glory to God in the highest . . . " My spiritual stocking received the image of a singing angel.

"He will save His people from their sins" (Matthew 1:21). In my mind I moved ahead to Christ's adult ministry and His death. His suffering and crucifixion bought my salvation. I wondered how anyone could do that much for me. I am not worthy of Christ's attention, much less His total life-and-death commitment. I whispered, "Thank You, Jesus," as I put a cross into my bulging stocking.

But I couldn't stop with the cross. I moved ahead to the empty tomb, and once again, a piercing joy took hold of me. Because of Christ's triumph on Easter, I received forgiveness and eternal life. ME! I'm going to be in heaven with the almighty God.

My spiritual stocking was now overflowing with God's gifts, and I added the final one, peace, on top. I felt God's peace flowing through me and realized all of my busy-ness is not important. I knelt in worship at the birthplace of the Prince of Peace.

Join me?

Prayer:

Dear Infant Jesus, You were born to reconcile me to God. Keep me always mindful of Your overwhelming love. And let me rejoice in the blessing of sharing that love with my students. In Your adorable name. Amen.

Homework:

Dig out a Christmas stocking and fill it with your own spiritual inventory of blessings from God.

The Children's Christmas Service

Reading: Luke 2:11–12

Today in the town of David a Savior has been born to you; He is Christ the Lord. This will be a sign to you: You will find a baby wrapped in cloth and lying in a manger.

Thank You, God. You got us through another children's Christmas service, I prayed silently as we drove home on Christmas Eve.

Every fall as we begin preparations, I vow to keep the message of Christ's birth in the forefront. But as November rolls around, the DETAILS intrude.

First, we have to agree on what type of service to prepare. That's not easy. Our staff includes traditionalists and modern thinkers, musicians and dramatists and pragmatists. After several debates, we reach a grudging compromise.

Remember the message!

Next comes the assigning of parts and songs for each class to learn. Do we want individual recitations or groups? Which classes will sing together? Should we plan costumes? Our discussions seem to overshadow the main theme of the service.

Remember the message.

Now for the rehearsals. The first couple of run-throughs are naturally rough, and the children pick up our tension. Soon we see glimpses of promise, but a lot of work still lies ahead. Will those kids EVER know their parts? Don't their parents realize they have to help?

Remember the message?

The final rehearsal is not a triumph, but you decide it's out of your hands. In fact, you say with some relief, "Well, God, it's up to You. I've done all I can."

Remember the . . .

Christmas Eve arrives and you're just sure you're too nervous to go. But Someone tugs on your spiritual shirtsleeve and you get there on time. Dozens of youngsters fidget as you glance around the room.

"Where's Tommy? It's almost time to go in."

Just then he races in, shouting, "I'm sorry. I had a football game and I really needed a shower."

With a huge sigh of relief, you hurry him into his costume and get the procession started.

What did I forget?

Oh, yes, the message. You feel God's love sweep the congregation as Tommy, halo slightly askew, steps up to the shepherds and proclaims, "Do not be afraid. I bring you good news of great joy . . . "

Prayer:

Father, forgive me for getting in Your way. Too often I think it all depends on me, and I forget that I am Your tool to lead others to salvation. Humbly, I beg Your forgiveness. To You alone belongs the glory! Amen.

Homework:

Take careful stock of your teaching. Is God your leader or your last resort? Pray about it.

The Master Key

Reading: Isaiah 33:5–6

The Lord is exalted, for He dwells on high; He will fill Zion with justice and righteousness. He will be the sure foundation for your times, a rich store of salvation and wisdom and knowledge; the fear of the Lord is the key to this treasure.

There was a timid knock at the door. I looked up and called, "Come in." But the door didn't open. Instead, a small, perplexed face looked through the window and jiggled the knob. It was one of my students, and she couldn't get back into the classroom.

The custodian opens the doors each day, but he leaves the knobs locked. It's up to the teachers to unlock them later, and obviously I hadn't that day. I scurried to do so.

When Ryan got in, she just looked at me and shook her head. "Boy, all I can say is I'm glad you're not in charge of unlocking heaven's doors."

After our laughter died down, I realized how right she was. What if God had given me or any other human the job of re-opening heaven?

Several approaches come to mind. I might try a "What's-in-it-for-me?" approach and bargain with God to work out a good deal. Someone else might try the oily, wheedling "just-do-it-this-one-time" approach, and we could all slide in on the oil slick he leaves. Another approach might be the military plan: "Let's blast down the gates and charge on in." Most of us, though, would probably have the "I-can't-therefore-I-won't-try" attitude.

There is one more possibility. And it's the plan God followed—the "how-much-is-it-going-to-cost-Me?" approach. It would have been impossible for us to come up with the price. The only way heaven's doors could open again was for God to "spend" His Son's life. Jesus' precious blood bought salvation for us. It cost God the Father a staggering amount to watch His Son pay the price for our sin.

But, praise God, it didn't end there. Jesus rose victorious and opened heaven's gates wide for all Christians to march through. Ryan knows and believes this. I do too. Jesus doesn't just hold the keys to heaven. He IS the master key to heaven.

Prayer:
Savior, I owe You everything. You bought me back from eternal death with Your own death and resurrection. Strengthen my faith daily and bring me safely home to Your eternal care. Through You alone. Amen.

Homework:
Role play with your class the approaches to salvation mentioned in the devotion. Discuss why only the last one is an effective way to get into heaven.

God's Crayons

Reading: Psalm 8:3–4

When I consider Your heavens, the work of Your fingers, the moon and the stars, which You have set in place, what is man that You are mindful of him, the son of man that You care for him?

Done. Finished. Complete. My twelfth year of teaching was over. I had just promoted another group of students, and I was thinking back over the year just ended. My mind whirled through a kaleidoscope of images that God had colored for me:

- The brilliant blue of a fall afternoon; Suzie's round eyes; Nancy's moods.
- The gray of low winter clouds; puddles; Larry's grief-filled eyes and subsequent art project.
- The purples of distant mountain peaks; irises; Paul's favorite marker; and Stacey's skirt and sweater.
- The yellow of lemons; dandelions; Jean's pencils; and Jason's project on bees.
- The rough brown of tree bark; squishy mud; Abe Lincoln log cabins; earnest, love-drawn crosses.
- The orange of tabby cats; oranges in lunches.
- The pink of carnations and hair ribbons.
- The green of the first leaves; a forest canopy; Lynn's snake; and Vic's frog.
- The silver slice of moon; the silver flash of Jenny's braces when she smiles.
- The white cotton-ball clouds; snow bunnies; Greg's face when he became ill.
- The black velvet hug of a spring night; Iowa soil.
- The red of American Beauty roses; the fleeting glimpse of a scarlet cardinal; and the blood my Savior shed.

You DO have some box of crayons, Lord!

Prayer:

Dear Creator, You looked at the world at its beginning and pronounced it very good. Thank You for the beauty of Your earth and Your beautiful children whom You entrusted to me to teach. Guide and guard them always. Keep them close to You and strong in their faith in Jesus, our risen Redeemer. In His name. Amen.

Homework:

Use a child's box of crayons and list your own favorite images of God's colorful world.